WATERS OF LIFE
FROM CONECUH RIDGE

THE CONECUH SERIES

WATERS OF LIFE

FROM

CONECUH RIDGE

THE CLYDE MAY STORY

WADE HALL

NEWSOUTH BOOKS

Montgomery | Louisville

NewSouth Books
P.O. Box 1588
Montgomery, AL 36102

Library of Congress Cataloging-in-Publication Data
ISBN-13: 978-1-60306-012-7
ISBN-10: 1-60306-012-X

Design by Randall Williams
Printed in the United States of America

THE CONECUH SERIES

CELEBRATING DIVERSITY IN THE SOUTH

Like the springs that unite to form the headwaters of the Conecuh River near Union Springs, Alabama, this series seeks to bring together the South's many traditions and cultures, celebrating at once our differences and our commonality.

IN MEMORY OF

CLYDE MAY

AND

W. H. "JABO" HALL

WHO KNEW A THING OR TWO ABOUT
THE WATERS OF LIFE

(whiskey, from Scots/Irish
Gaelic *uisge beatha,* "water of life")

CONTENTS

WATERS OF LIFE
FROM CONECUH RIDGE

This story of Clyde May and his family is based on interviews conducted by Wade Hall with Kenny May in Louisville, Kentucky, during the spring and summer of 2000 and the fall of 2002. It was transcribed from audio tapes by Gregg Swem and rewritten and reformatted by Wade Hall. The narrator is Kenny May.

Lewis Clyde May (1922–1990).

I

The May Family
of Conecuh Ridge

Daddy used to say that our hardscrabble farm was only good for growing pine trees, sandspurs, peanuts, younguns, and fine moonshine whiskey. He never made much off the first four products, but he did right well on number five. I reckon I ought to know. I spent many a day and night in the deep piney woods of southeast Alabama helping him make moonshine.

My name is Kenneth Lewis May. I'm named after my daddy, Lewis Clyde May; but I'm not a junior. Part of my name came from one of Daddy's Army buddies in World War II named Kenneth.

I was born and grew up in Bullock County, Alabama, in the Almeria community in the shadow of Macedonia Baptist Church. Almeria community was named for a school, which was named for a place in the Bible. It's between Hooks Cross Roads and Beans Cross Roads. There never has been very much at either place except for a few houses and a couple of stores. Mr. Seals Hooks's store has been abandoned for years and is about to fall in and be covered with kudzu vines. If decay and the kudzu don't do it in, it'll eventually fall down the cliff right behind the store. There's a big ravine back there on the edge of Conecuh Ridge. I've never been down there, but I imagine it's

Mary Cynthia and Clyde May, about 1943, before he shipped out to the Pacific Theater of World War II.

filled with all kinds of wild animals and serpents—and maybe a few missing cars and bleached bones.

I was born in a frame house on an unpaved lane called Rabbit Road. Mr. Jim Rotton, who moved down the road from us when I was a little boy, said it was named by Allen Dykes, who used to run a county road grader before the road was paved. He lived over near Bethel and didn't like to come way over here just to grade off our road, so he told Carl Green, our road commissioner, "Carl, ain't no use to grade that road. Ain't nothing gone travel it—even if it was blacktopped—unless it's a damned rabbit." After that, everybody started calling it Rabbit Road. There were a few more people that lived on the road—Miss Belle McInnis, Mr. Jim's brother Carl Rotton, Mr. Vivian Herndon—but you might say it was never heavily populated.

Daddy bought our homeplace in 1950, the year I was

born. Before that, he had rented the Sellers Place right next to Macedonia Church which was owned by Dr. Sumpter Reynolds. The Reynoldses and the Sellerses were kin some way. Dr. Reynolds was a veterinarian in Troy, but he was a native of Bullock County and he loved his old homeplace. He had a brother named John Lem Reynolds who lived diagonally across from Miss Mattie Clyde Brooks's store at Beans Cross Roads. He was a huge, heavy-set fellow—probably weighed four hundred pounds.

Anyway, that's where my family lived before I was born. Dr. Reynolds has been gone a long time, but his daughter Eulayla Holson—her husband is a retired Army colonel—lives in Troy. She was one of four children, and she still owns about two hundred acres of land right behind Miss Mattie Clyde's store. I think her brothers and sisters have sold off all their land.

It was the first time my daddy had ever owned any land. He first bought a hundred and ninety acres from Mr. Ernest Roughton, who was Mr. Raymond Roughton's brother. Later on, he bought forty more acres from Mr. Vivian Herndon and then sixty acres from Miss Belle McInnis. So we had a farm of almost three hundred acres, which was a big spread for us. Of course, it was very poor sandy land and didn't grow very much, as Daddy said, except for a pretty good crop of peanuts and children. Children can thrive on just about any kind of soil, and peanuts love sandy land. Sandy soil is well-drained and it's easy to dig peanuts and shake the dirt off them. You should try to separate peanuts from clay soil! They just won't come out of the ground when that clay gets hard. But sandy land just turns those peanuts loose without any fuss. Sandy soil was also pretty good for growing corn, but you couldn't get half a bale of cotton to an acre.

I don't know what he paid for the last two parcels of land, but I did hear him say that he paid thirty-five hundred dollars for the first hundred and ninety acres. That was less than twenty dollars an acre and it included a house and a barn and a fenced pasture. It was one of those dogtrot houses, with an open hallway in the middle, where dogs and varmints and children could run through. It was a pretty good house for the price and for the place and time. Before we moved out, it got a little crowded.

You see, I was the fourth of eight children, four boys and four girls. The oldest one is my sister Lenita, who married Donald Hall. The next is Zelda, then comes my brother Charles, who married Linda Bassett. But nobody knows him by Charles. He answers to Spooky. Two years later I came along, followed in five years by a set of twins, Jack, who's not married, and Jill, who married Art Hancock. Three years later Debbie came. She is mentally handicapped and lives at the homeplace with brother Jack. They live together in the brick house that Daddy built us when I was ten. Spooky tore down the old dogtrot house and built himself a modern house on the homeplace site. Some of us have never completely forgiven Spooky for doing this. I wish we still had the old place. It would bring back a lot of good memories.

But several of us Mays still live on Rabbit Road—Debbie and Jack, Spooky and his family, Jill and her family, and Billy's family. Now we've started a new generation on Rabbit Road—Spooky and Zelda both have children living there. We just about have Mr. Jim Rotton's place surrounded.

I love all my brothers and sisters, but Debbie is special to all of us. Because of her needs, she has to have somebody with her all the time, so Ruby Kilpatrick, Gilbert Hall's daughter,

Mary and Clyde May with Debbie.

comes over five days a week to be with her and housekeep. Ruby stayed with Mama until she died of a stroke; then she just stayed on to help with Debbie. She's got six children of her own, but she loves Debbie like her own daughter. She lives in Corinth and goes home every evening and comes back in the morning when Jack leaves for work. Debbie can bathe and feed herself but she can't cook. She's got a fantastic memory but she can't read or write. She lives in her own world and has no sense of reality. She's never been institutionalized—and never will be, not if her seven brothers and sisters can help it. Each of us takes a turn to oversee Debbie for a week at the time. When my week comes, I make sure somebody—me or somebody else—is with Debbie when Ruby or Jack is not there—especially on the weekends. Sometimes I take her to

The Mays with the older children—Lenita and Spooky in front, Zelda and Kenny behind the door.

my house in Troy, but when it begins to get dark she wants to go home; and I take her back and spend the night if Jack is not there. About the only place she'll spend the night is at Lenita and Donald's house. They take up a lot of time with her, and she's real fond of them.

Well, that's all of us, except for the youngest, Billy, who is twenty-one years younger than Lenita, and who is married to Jane Youngblood. That's almost a whole generation of difference between the oldest and the youngest. Mama had two grandchildren who were older than Billy. Because he was born to Mama and Daddy so late in life, Billy was their "special" baby—and they spoiled him. By this time, they were more able to give him material things, so Spooky nicknamed him "the silver spoon kid."

I'm glad I am part of a large family. I can't imagine not having any one of my brothers and sisters. Each one is special to me in a different way. Of course, we've had a few fusses and fights, but that's normal. At different times, I've felt closer to different ones. At one time it was Zelda, who has always been so protective and nurturing—like Daddy. Another time it was Spooky or someone else. As I've grown older, I've become closer to Lenita. She is six years older than me, and that made a lot of difference when I was a little boy and making a big nuisance of myself by tagging along after her all the time. But now that we're both in our fifties, the age difference doesn't seem to matter; and we find that we have a lot of common interests.

We were not all at home at the same time, though at one time seven of us were together. By the time Billy came along, however, Lenita and Zelda had married and moved out. But even as we started going our own ways, we continued to see

Family picture, 1967. Top: Zelda, Kenny, Spooky, and Lenita. Bottom: Jack, Billy, Clyde May, Debbie (standing), Mary May, and Jill.

each other frequently at family get-togethers. These family "get-togethers" happened as frequently as every Sunday. We all just naturally gravitated toward Mama's dinner table each Sunday—a tradition that continued until her death. Sometimes there were almost as many cars in their yard on Sunday as there were at the church. (By the way, "dinner" at our house was the noontime meal. Our evening meal was called "supper.")

With such a large family, there was a lot of work to be done; and all of us had our chores in and around the house. Mama supervised the girls in the house and garden, and Daddy had charge of us boys with the farming and outside work. When I was small, we did a lot of row cropping, and I remember picking a little cotton and shaking a few peanuts.

One time my love of mischief almost got me into a lot of trouble. It was early one summer and we were side dressing the corn with guano fertilizer. Spooky and I were playing around on the fertilizer wagon at the edge of the field. Daddy had several extra plow points in the wagon in case one broke and had to be replaced. They were heavy iron pieces shaped and sharpened to open up the soil. They could also open up a person's flesh and bone. I was playing with one of the points when I decided it would be fun to hold it over Spooky's head and pretend to drop it. Well, I held it over his head and it slipped from my hand and hit Spooky right on his head and cut it wide open. When Daddy saw what had happened, he grabbed Spooky and ran to the house and cranked up the car and rushed to the doctor in Troy. They sewed Spooky up and he eventually got well. It's a wonder I hadn't killed him! That was one of the many times Mama beat the Dickens out of me. Spooky was a tough little boy and so was I. We both survived. I never played with plow points again. When I was about seven, we quit planting cotton and peanuts and didn't do much field work any more. We did, however, continue with Daddy's branch work. More about that later.

Clyde May with some of his brothers and sisters. Clockwise from top left: Buck, Clyde, Mattie Lou, Catherine, and Nell.

2

Growing Up on Rabbit Road

I never got interested in my family history until a few years ago. It just seemed like our people had always lived in Bullock County. Before he died, Mr. Hobson Roughton, one of our neighbors who lived over at High Ridge, did some genealogy on the May family and found out that we came over from Ireland sometime in the 1700s and settled in Sumpter, South Carolina; then in the early 1800s we started moving west and eventually made it to just east of Columbus, Georgia. Right before the Civil War, some of us moved over here to Bullock County, which was then a part of Pike County. Then some of us moved on to Mississippi and settled in Canton. A few of them got as far as Texas. To this day we have identified kinfolks scattered all the way from South Carolina to Texas.

One time, when I was selling plants for Bonnie Plant Farm up at Sardis, near Union Springs, I had a customer in Canton, Mississippi, named Robert May, who ran a little grocery store. One night I went by his store and found him with half a bottle of bourbon and in a talkative mood. He said, "Kenny, don't you think we might be kin?" I said, "Well, Mr. Robert, we might be." He said, "My folks came from South Carolina, settled for a while in Bullock County, Alabama, and then moved over here to Mississippi." I said, "Yes, sir, it seems to me that we are likely kin—somewhere way back there." Over that second

This is the only known picture of Clyde May (left) with his mother,
Annie Lillis. The other children, from left, Buck, Nell, and Mattie
Lou, were actually his mother's younger siblings, and thus were his
uncle and aunts. But after his mother's death, Clyde was raised
by his maternal grandparents and he knew his younger aunts and
uncles as sisters and brothers.

half bottle of bourbon, we decided that we were kin.

Yes, sir, my family has lived in Bullock County a long time
and is connected to a lot of different families. My maternal
grandmother Victoria was a Bates and had eleven brothers
and sisters. The oldest one was Mr. Johnson Bates and the
youngest one was Uncle Doug Bates. He's the one who killed
himself down behind Mt. Zion Church in the gas truck that
he drove. Two of his sisters, Aunt Minnie Ree Brooks and
Aunt Josephine Pritchett, lived to be over a hundred. We're
also kin to the Outlaw family through Grandmother Bates. My
mother, who was also from the Macedonia community, was a

Petty—Mary Cynthia Petty—the only girl of six children born to my grandparents, William and Victoria Petty. They were sharecroppers and lived on one of the Sellerses' farms.

Daddy was born out of wedlock to Annie May, a daughter of Grandfather Charlie May and Grandmother Hattie May. His mother died when he was five years old and his grandparents adopted and raised him. He called them Mama and Pappa and when he referred to his real mother he called her "My Mama."

I think it bothered him that he was illegitimate. I believe he always felt that he was sometimes shunned and didn't fit in because of his birth but he never said a word about it. He did tell me once, just weeks before he died, that he always felt that he was taking food from the others' mouths. Times were hard in those days. The Depression was causing tremendous hardships. People were going to bed hungry, and Daddy felt

Lenita, Zelda, and Spooky with Grandmama Petty in the chicken coop.

like he was a burden to his grandparents. You see, they still had other young children at home also. Although they loved him as their own, he often felt that he was an intruder. Until their deaths, Daddy tried to show them his appreciation for all they had done for him. When he joined the Army, he had a portion of his allotment sent to them, and the rest sent to Mama. Grandfather Charlie died before Daddy returned from the war. Both Grandmother Hattie and one of Daddy's older brothers lived with us on the Rabbit Road until their deaths.

Daddy and Mama made a home for several of their kin during their lifetimes. At one time or another, my two grandmothers, my uncle, a great-aunt, and Mama's baby brother Hubert lived with us. Hubert was only a few years older than us, and we loved having another "kid" in the house. He was the first in the family to become one of Daddy's "assistants" in the family business. Daddy loved Hubert like his own, and we all still have a special place in our hearts for him.

Daddy was a strict disciplinarian but a good father to all his children. I remember very few times when he ever whipped any one of us, but he seldom had to. We knew where the boundaries were, and we never crossed him or the boundaries. He had some kind of force over us. He only had to tell us one time to do something, and we did it. I guess you could say that he ruled his family with an iron hand that could beat the slop out of us. But we knew he was foolish about every one of us, and we never doubted his love. Now I realize how lucky we were to have him as a father. Even when I was a boy, I never envied other children. For that time and that place, I know I had a storybook childhood.

Of course, by some standards we were poor. But so was

everyone else in our community. We had as much—maybe more—than our neighbors. We always had decent, clean clothes and shoes to wear, our own house to live in, and plenty to eat. When Mama set the table for a meal, she always put out more than we needed, in case we had unexpected visitors—which we often did. Even if the main dish was peas and cornbread, we always had enough to share. Like everybody else, we grew most of our food. Every year Daddy had a big garden and

Mary Cynthia Petty as a girl, holding her brother next to friend Bo Reeves.

Mary Cynthia Petty May (1922–1997).

patches of corn and peas and butterbeans, which Mama and my sisters would can for the cold months. For a long time Spooky and I milked three cows every morning, which gave us plenty of milk and butter. We always had a calf or a pig to slaughter and pack into the deep-freeze.

I can't give all the credit to Daddy. Mama did a large share of raising us. Daddy may have spared the rod but Mama didn't. She whipped the tar out of me more times than I can count. I don't think I was a bad boy, but I did manage to get into a lot of trouble. And when I did, Mama was waiting with a fresh switch from the sugarberry tree across the road. They made the best switches because they wouldn't break. Sometimes, to add insult to injury, she'd make us go cut our own switches. But she never needed any help in applying it to our rear ends or the fleshy parts of our legs—the body parts that wouldn't leave any permanent injury. Mama didn't mean to hurt us, just to discipline us. Her message got through to us—at least, for a while.

I knew I had a good home life and never once thought about running away. Where could I have found anything better? Daddy was generous to us children to a fault, especially at Christmas time. It was always a big occasion in our family. Every Christmas we all got gobs of stuff—from BB guns to

Lenita, Uncle Thelton, Clyde May, and Zelda at Christmas time. Christmas dolls are on the truck bumper.

shotguns, from wagons to bicycles, from dolls to storybooks, from new coats and shoes to candied raisins, English walnuts and Brazil nuts. I remember Mama telling that one Christmas, after she and Daddy had made sure we all had plenty of toys, she and Daddy looked outside to find us playing with a piece of rope. She said Daddy commented, "Damn, Shug, we could have saved some money by just giving each one of them a plow rope." I think Daddy wanted us to have a big Christmas to make up for the poor Christmases he had as a boy. On his Christmas mornings, he was happy to get an orange or an apple and a few nuts. I think the best Christmas he ever had as a child was when he got a small pocket knife.

He was always trying to make sure we got what we needed. Here's another throwback, I believe, to his own youth. When we got married and began to have children, Daddy always insisted on buying each child its first pair of shoes. When my oldest son was nine or ten months old and about ready to start walking, Daddy came to my house and announced, "I'm going to buy Tommy his first pair of shoes." And he did. And to my knowledge, he did that for all his grandchildren.

As much as I know Daddy and Mama loved their children and took care of us, they never showed their love publicly. They just didn't make a display of their affection for us. But that was part of the culture we lived in. I never saw other parents in our community showing their love in public either. Every day they worked and sacrificed for us and showed their love in so many ways—from the good food that Mama always put on the table to the great times we had with games and sports that Daddy encouraged us to play. But at home, Daddy enjoyed playing with us. I remember him playing hide-and-seek and other children's games. And he always got a kick out of popping us on the butt with the twisted corner of a towel. We'd squeal, he would laugh, and Mama would fuss because we were so noisy.

Mama was a wonderful cook, and she never had to use a cookbook. In fact, I don't think she even had one. She cooked from memory and from the heart. Like most Southern cooks, she fried everything she could. And she made the best buttermilk biscuits I ever ate. And cakes. She made cakes for us and for everybody in the neighborhood. Red velvet was her trademark cake, but she also made delicious German chocolate cake, fruitcake—just about any kind you can mention. It was all country cooking, so we didn't have much variety, and, of course, we never heard of ethnic foods like Chinese or Mexican or French. Our meats were mostly pork, beef, fish, chicken,

Snow was rare in southeast Alabama; but when it came, everybody had a good time. Here is Clyde May, surrounded by his children, nieces, and nephews, enjoying the scarce treat.

and game that the men would bring in from the woods. We had fresh vegetables in the summer and canned and frozen vegetables in the winter. I think the women, especially, spent most of the summer picking and shelling and cooking and canning peas and butterbeans and tomatoes and tomato relish. We certainly had plenty to eat at any season of the year.

We worked hard, but we always had time to play. When I was a boy we played some marbles, but not like my daddy's generation. To them, it was a serious sport. It taught them one of life's basic lessons: You win some and you lose some. Once, when Daddy was a third grader at a small, one-room school in Almeria Community, he almost got into a lot of trouble. Some of the boys played marbles each day at recess or lunchtime. Daddy and his older brother Buck wanted to play, but didn't have any marbles. One of them came up with a wonderful idea. The desks in their classroom had lift-up seats, meaning each seat came equipped with nice shiny steel "marbles." Daddy and Uncle Buck sneaked back into the school after everyone else had left and took the steel ball bearings out of several desks. The next morning they were ready to win at marbles, knowing that their steel marbles would beat anything else out there.

But when they got to school, the teacher was in a rage because many of the desk seats came apart when the children sat down. Daddy and Uncle Buck just looked at each other, too frightened to admit what they had done. They each carried those ball bearings around in their pockets all day, then threw them in the woods on the way home from school. I don't guess they ever confessed that they had torn up the desks at school.

We played hide-and-go-seek, which we just called "hidin'."

But mostly we boys played ball—softball and baseball—every chance we had. We took over one of Mr. Wilbur Sykes's cow pastures and turned it into a makeshift baseball field and called it Happy Valley. Because it had so many tree stumps scattered all over it, we also nicknamed it Stump Stadium. Sometimes we'd run into a stump and get the breath knocked out of us, but usually we dodged the stumps and our opponents and managed to get home to score a run. Sometimes we'd play softball, but we considered that mainly a game for girls and old people. And we played a little tag football, but baseball was our grand passion. We could play it from sunup until it got too dark to see the ball or the bat.

I also had a bicycle and rode it until I wore the wheels off. Rabbit Road was sand and dirt in those days, but the road from Hooks Cross Roads to Beans Cross Road was paved, and I wore my tires and myself out riding that pavement. Down below our house on Rabbit Road was a long hill that led down to Flat Creek, which had a vibrating wooden bridge over it. Sometimes I'd hit that bridge doing thirty miles an hour, with no brakes and no way to stop except going up the next hill. I was going like thunder and coming in on a wing and a prayer.

3

School Time, the Fourth of July Singing, and Mama's Cooking

Work, play, and school took up most of my time when I was a boy. When I started to school in 1956, we had moved up to Aberfoil, where Daddy was operating some big chicken houses. That was about when the poultry business first hit Bullock County. The next year we moved back to Rabbit Road, and I went from the second through the eighth grades at Inverness School. In 1964, when I was supposed to start the ninth grade in Union Springs, which had just been integrated, Daddy sent us to Clayton High School in Barbour County. I went through the eleventh grade at Clayton and then transferred to a private school near Tuskegee, Macon Academy, where I finished high school. Most of my brothers and sisters finished high school, which was a huge advancement over my parents' generation, when a lot of people—black and white—couldn't even read or write.

When integration came, Daddy worked hard to send us to private schools because he believed that we couldn't get a good education in a mixed school. It wasn't that he disliked black people at all. He always had good relations with them. He treated them fairly, and they liked him. It just took him a long time to accept the social changes that were headed our way. For years Daddy looked up to George Wallace as a hero, but before he died, he had changed his mind. "Son," he confessed to me one day, "I've been wrong about George. First and foremost, he's one shrewd politician."

After I finished high school, I went to Troy State for a while. Daddy wanted me to be the first one of our family to finish college, and I know I disappointed him when I dropped out. But I knew that I was wasting my time and Daddy's money, so I left. For some people, college is not a good fit. Nobody in my family of my generation finished college. But the next generation is different. We already have several college graduates—Zelda's youngest son Casey, who graduated in math from Troy State several years ago; Spooky's son David, who is also a Troy State graduate; and my son Tony, who graduated from Troy State in math.

When I got a little size on me, I began to notice girls. I had a few little girlfriends when I was growing up—down in Clayton and in Union Springs and at Macon Academy. But I was not really serious about anybody until I met my first wife, Kathy Krieger. She was a dental hygienist in Troy. She is the mother of our two sons. But we grew apart and got divorced. Then I married my present wife, Kim, who was also divorced. We had known each other distantly when we were married to our other spouses, but we didn't get to know each other until we both were spending a lot of time at the same ball park in Troy with our kids. We discovered we had a lot in common and began spending time together away from the ball park as well, and finally we got married. I was so fortunate to find her. She is just as sweet as she is pretty. Between us, we have five kids. I have two sons and three stepchildren, and they're all good. We never have any trouble with them. I'm having a ball with my life now.

Macedonia was our church, and most of us were baptized and became members. We had church services—or, preaching, as we called it—throughout the year; but our big day was the Fourth of July Singing. It was an all-day gathering that started soon after the Civil War. It included a celebration of Independence Day as well as preaching and singing, especially. The music was an old-fashioned kind called Sacred Harp or fa-so-la singing, and people would sing the notes, then the words. A lot of people in my family learned that kind of singing, but I never did. The Fourth of July Singing rated second only to Christmas in holiday importance in my family. No matter how short money was or how hard the times were, Daddy and Mama always managed to find the money to buy each child new clothes, head to foot, for the occasion. And they spent days preparing food to take to the church.

Clyde May being baptized in 1955 by the Rev. J. W. Hardin, pastor of Macedonia Baptist Church; Hardin had served in CCC camp with May in the early 1940s.

For us children, the main attraction at the singing was all the barbecued pork and fried chicken and the endless bowls of vegetables and plates of cakes and pies that families would bring and spread on long tables outside at dinnertime. There was also an ice cream stand where for a nickel or a dime we could get a dish of vanilla ice cream. The celebration lasted all day long; and from time to time you could see men slipping off into the woods to take quick swallows of moonshine whiskey—some of it, I'm sure, made by my daddy and his sons.

Daddy always brought a lot of barbecued meat, which he had cooked the day before at a barbecue pit down at the old Almeria schoolhouse. Sometimes he would barbecue a whole pig and sometimes he would use Boston butts and hams. In the wintertime, Daddy would sometimes kill a hog, stretch him over a pit in our backyard and barbecue him slowly over hickory coals—maybe sixteen to eighteen hours—and invite the whole community. Just about everybody came.

Daddy was sociable but he never spent much time away from home. He'd go any distance anywhere with you if you could get him back home in time to sleep in his own bed that night. One time, when I was working for Bonnie Plant Farm over in Mississippi, he agreed to come over and help me for a week or so. Before that week was up, I could tell he was getting mighty homesick. He didn't like any of the food we ate. Just before we left for home, we were sitting in this little café eating and he pushed his plate back and said, "Boy, I sure will be glad to get back home and get some of your Mama's cooking. If your Mama put something like this in front of me, I'd raise hell. I ain't had nothing decent to eat since I left Alabama." I know he missed Mama's cooking, and I know he also missed Mama. But, of course, he'd never say that out loud. Maybe he thought it would have been a sign of weakness to admit that he loved or needed her.

I'd never seen him hug and kiss Mama in public before, but when we got home, he couldn't seem to take his hands off her. But that only lasted for a few days, and then he went back to taking her for granted.

4

DADDY IN WAR AND PEACE

Except for the time he was off in World War II, he and Mama were always together. He was in the Army and came home on leave in April of 1943 when they got married. Late that fall he was sent to the South Pacific and didn't see his first child, who was born in May of 1944, until she was fourteen months old. When he came home, Lenita didn't know who he was. She was scared to death of him, and it hurt his feelings for a while.

He spent about a year and a half in the infantry in Guam and Okinawa. He was in a lot of combat and got wounded in both feet by machine gun fire. He and one of his buddies were going down a hill on Guam when they got hit. His buddy got shot in the belly, and they were both evacuated to a hospital. As they were leaving, they were given different colored tags. A blue tag meant you stayed and would be sent back to the front lines. A red tag meant that you'd be sent home and discharged. Daddy knew his buddy was in worse shape than he was and would be sent home. But he was wrong. It was Daddy who was given the red tag and sent home. We still have the Purple Heart he was awarded. He had trouble with his feet until the day he died.

Daddy didn't like to talk about his war service. He said it was about fighting and killing, and he did a lot of both. That's all he would say. As I said, he told me that I was named Kenneth after another one of his buddies. "It was on Okinawa," he said, "and we were in the middle of some bad fighting. I saw him fall and ran over to him and said, 'What can I do?' He said, 'I need a drink of water.' So I took him in my arms and held my canteen up to his lips. He took one swallow and died. I promised him right then and there that if I ever had any sons, I'd name one of them Kenneth."

My daddy wasn't perfect. I don't think he ever treated Mama right. No, I don't mean that he ever hit her physically. It's just that he wanted things done his way; and when they didn't go his way, he sulked. He pouted. He gave Mama the silent treatment. He'd go for days and days without even speaking to her. And another thing: he never complimented her. He never praised her. And if he ever consulted her before making a decision, I never knew it. After I was grown and had gotten bolder, I asked him, "Daddy, why don't you treat Mama better?" All he said was, "Son, there are a lot of things you don't know and won't ever know." So that was it. I never pushed him again. Then after Daddy died, I began to see that Mama could be as pushy and demanding and domineering as he was. I realized that if Daddy hadn't dominated her, she would have dominated him. It was her nature. Now, the older I get the smarter my daddy gets. He was the man in the family; and if anyone was going to dominate, it would be him. I know, too, that he would have fought a circular saw for Mama, but he was going to do it his way.

A lot of people had a lot of respect for Daddy. You take Lanier Beasley. He started out as a school teacher but decided he could make more money cutting hair. So he opened a barber shop on the square in Troy and cut Daddy's hair for a long

Clyde May with his sister Mattie Lou, who also served in the Armed Forces during World War II.

time. He still cuts mine. One day right after Daddy died, I was sitting in the chair having my hair cut, and he said, "Kenny, your daddy was a fine man. I know he ruled his family with a strong hand, but I also know that the hand that might knock the hell out of you if you disobeyed him was the same hand that wouldn't allow anybody else to touch you."

Yes, Daddy had a few faults. Another one is that he would never admit that he was wrong about anything—even when he knew he was wrong. And I never heard him apologize for anything he ever did—except for one time. When I was a senior at Macon Academy, I wanted to play football. I even went out for it and made the team. It meant I had to stay after school and somebody had to pick me up and take me home. It wouldn't have been a big sacrifice for him, and he knew how much it meant to me. But he made me quit the team so I could drive the bus home. Years later, when my youngest brother was playing football, Daddy and I were watching him one night from the sidelines, when Daddy said, "I'm so proud of Billy. He's a good ball player." And I said, "He sure is. I wish I could have played football when I was in high school." And he said, "Son, I do, too. I should have let you play. I'm sorry. I was wrong."

Daddy was a hard disciplinarian, but one time he acted too quickly. It's a story about Lenita and Zelda and a whipping he gave them for something they didn't do. One day the girls, who were about six and eight years old, got off the school bus and were walking down the dirt road toward home, which was about a quarter of a mile away. As they passed old man John McInnis's house, they were playing around in the sand beds and stopped to watch him cut his hedgerow right by the road. Now, we didn't have hedges around our yard, and they were

Clyde May with family members before he left for service during WW II. From left, Clarence, Nell, Beuna, Clyde May, Matte Lou, Grandmama Hattie, and Grandaddy Charlie. Aunt Beuna's son, Ferrell, is kneeling.

curious to see what he was doing. Just as they walked up, he left and went out back to his garden to shoo some chickens out and went on in the house. Well, Nita and Zelda played in the sand a few minutes and then went on home. About an hour later, Mr. John walked up to our house and said to Daddy, "Your girls have stolen my hedge shears! I was cutting my hedge and had to leave for a few minutes and when I came back, the girls were gone and so were my shears." So Daddy said, "Well, I'll take care of them."

The girls protested their innocence. Lenita said, "Daddy, we don't know anything about his hedge shears. We don't even have a hedge to cut. We were just watching him cut his. I've never had a pair of shears in my hands. Daddy, please believe us. We didn't take his shears." But he didn't believe them and made them walk with him all the way back to the old man's house looking for the shears in the ditches on both sides of the road in case they had thrown them down. They found nothing. But that proved nothing to him. So he took them home and beat the tar out of them.

A few days later, Mama had to go to the store and took Zelda and Lenita with her. As they were passing Mr. John's house, he ran out in the road and waved our car down. Mama stopped and Mr. John came to her widow and said, "Mrs. May, I want you to let these girls get out of your car and whip me just like their daddy whipped them. They didn't take my shears. They had fallen down inside the hedge, and I've just found them. They didn't steal anything of mine. I'm so sorry." Well, Lenita and Zelda were ready to get out and give him the lashing he deserved, but, of course, Mama wouldn't let 'em. It certainly taught that ornery, cranky old man a lesson. It also taught Daddy to trust his children a little more. Of course, if it had been Daddy driving our car to the store, he would probably have let the girls get out and whip the old man.

I consider my life very much a success now—personally and professionally. And I give a lot of the credit to my mama and daddy and to the work ethic they taught me. I used to think Daddy was working me to death, but now I'm thankful that he taught me the value and rewards of hard work. He used to say, "Son, I don't have much education; and I've had to work hard all my life. I hope you'll get enough education so you won't have to work as hard as I did, but in case you don't, at least you'll know how."

I worked for Bonnie Plant Farm, mostly traveling and distributing garden plants on my route in Mississippi. I learned a lot from the years I worked with Bonnie Plant Farm, but that's a young man's game, and I knew I couldn't hold out until retirement age. One important thing I learned from Bonnie was how the distributor-dealer business works. But I got tired of being on the road so much and away from home. So I quit and worked for one summer with Barber's Milk Company in Montgomery; then I decided I wanted a better job.

So one day I walked into the office of the Montgomery Seed Company and said, "I'd like to get in the seed business. Have y'all got any job openings?" An hour later I walked out with a new job. At first, I worked in the shipping department warehouse; then one of their salesmen retired and I took his job. I was with them for ten years. Montgomery Seed is a distributor of seeds grown mostly in the West—out in Oregon, Idaho, and California—then shipped in.

I started trading my own seed about eight years ago. I did most of my seed trading for Ron Rubin, a seed producer in California. Ron made my job easy; he is one of the most honest and respected men in the seed business. The main product we traded was Bermuda grass seed, which is grown in Southern California and Arizona. It's used mostly on the roadside, on the right of way; but it's also popular for pastures and lawns in the Deep South, that is, from Nashville on south. People in other parts of the country consider it a cuss word. "We don't want that weed up here," they say. "It stays brown too long." And truly it does go dormant in late fall, but in the South people overseed it with rye grass to provide a green lawn all winter. Then in the spring the rye will die back and the Bermuda grass will green up.

We also traded Bahia grass seed, which is grown mostly by contract growers in Alabama and Florida. Mr. Hick Sims from over at Simsville is one of our growers.

In all, I've had about twenty-three years in the seed business; and I've learned the ropes. It's pretty easy now because I've got my contacts and structures all set up, and I know how to run them. And most important, I've got a track record that people respect. I can call other people in the seed business and they know who I am. Here's an example. Bermuda grass seed isn't harvested until July, but we start booking or contracting the new crop months ahead. We'll call our distributors and say, "This is our program." That means our price, our terms, and so forth. Then we say, "How many pounds do you want?" To some distributors we'll sell a million pounds, and to some just a few hundred. People in the business trust us because they know that we'll deliver what we promise and deliver it on time. I'll probably stay in the seed business in some form or other for the rest of my life.

5

DADDY AND THE REVENUERS

Now I'm excited about another venture that is tied directly to my boyhood and my family, especially my daddy. I plan to distill and market a superior brand of whiskey patterned on the ingredients, techniques and standards that he used to make moonshine. The difference is that this time it will be legal. We will pay taxes. We will meet—and surpass—the production standards of the industry. And we will sell it openly to the public around the world. I think the story of my daddy's moonshining business—he called it "branch work"—will explain why I am so enthusiastic about this project and why I want to honor him by making his product available to a broader market. Let's go back again to my boyhood some thirty and forty years ago, back to when my mother and father were living and raising their eight children on the sandy soil of Rabbit Road near Conecuh Ridge in Bullock County, Alabama.

If you could ask him what is his greatest legacy, Daddy would say his children. But I think an important part of his legacy was the product that he made and sold illegally—the whiskey that made him and thousands of other men outlaws. I realize that part of his legacy is now in my hands, and I must be careful to do it justice. If I can show how Daddy made the best whiskey in South Alabama, that will be all the proof I need.

I can't remember a time when Daddy wasn't making moonshine whiskey. He never tried to keep it a secret from his family. He couldn't have, anyway. We all grew up knowing that he was moonshining but also knowing that we weren't supposed to tell anybody. I learned the trade at an early age. One time I almost let the cat out of the bag. A science experiment at Inverness School probably left a lot of people wondering who taught me how to make whiskey. In the eighth grade a friend, Donny Dunn, and I rigged up a still in our science lab. I brought some corn meal and sugar and yeast from home, and we fermented it and ran off maybe a cup full. We went through the whole process, from setting up the still to distilling the liquor. Donny took a swallow and said it tasted like whiskey. I took a whiff and it surely did smell like whiskey.

Of course, I had learned from my daddy—the way most moonshiners learned. When I was in the third grade, he took me with him to his whiskey still for the first time. I felt so excited and grown up. It was the biggest thrill I could imagine. It was a sign that I was becoming a man. As my father's helper, I enjoyed being taken into the company of men; but I knew that moonshining was a risky business. We were always afraid that the revenue agents would find our still, arrest us and send us to jail. After all, according to the law, we were doing something illegal. Of course, we didn't see it that way. It never bothered Daddy that he was doing something illegal. It bothered him only because he didn't want to get caught. The only thing he was doing wrong was not paying taxes on the whiskey. I think Daddy looked at whiskey-making like most of the men in our community and like most of our ancestors going back to Georgia and the Carolinas and Virginia and

Pennsylvania—even back to our people in Ireland and Scotland. It was a part of our folk culture, our tradition of making a living off the land—a heritage that allowed a man to provide for his family without interference from the government.

I think the poor farm land forced people into moonshining. The sandy soil we lived on could hardly support a family of ten people. So a man with a large family had to find other sources of income to supplement his meager farm profit. What better trade than one that had been a part of Irish and Scottish folklife for hundreds of years—spread from its roots in the waters of Scotland and Ireland across the Atlantic into the frontier cultures of the New World? It seemed to be a freeborn man's natural right to produce as much of the aqua vitae, the waters of life, as he needed for himself and perhaps for his neighbors. It was his right by inheritance and necessity. Why should he need permission and pay a tax on so ancient a product—on a birthright as basic as planting seed and harvesting corn or rye or wheat? Forget about the reforms of the nineteenth century that turned distilled spirits into the devil's poison. Go back beyond the preacher's raging against strong drink. Go back to a time when Jesus turned water into wine. Now consider that Kentucky bourbon was first distilled by a Baptist preacher. Now check the accounts and find that frontier preachers found their commissary sacks filled not only with chickens and corn and potatoes but with drams of sparkling water. Now look into the communion cup and see the holy wine that represents the sacred blood. Now tell me I don't have a right—a natural, God-given right—to produce this sacred water of life. That was the instinctive logic of the backwoods moonshiner.

Well, we didn't get rich from our illegal business; but we

got a good return on our investment. The initial setup cost was around three hundred dollars, which paid for a good-sized copper still and a supply of barrels for two dollars each. Both the still and the barrels lasted a long time. After the setup, our expenses were mainly the ingredients. The sugar, rye, gas and everything else would cost us about forty dollars for a run of whiskey. We'd run off about twenty gallons of whiskey, and we would sell it for five dollars a gallon, which gave us a hundred dollars on an investment of about forty dollars. A profit of sixty dollars was a lot of money to us in those days—especially for a couple of days' work. Down in our part of the country there wasn't anything else we could have done to make that much money. It would have been very hard for Daddy to support his family without moonshining. I don't think we would have starved or frozen to death, but we would certainly have had a lot less. I'm sure that Daddy was willing to risk his freedom in order to provide a better living for his family.

Some men in the business did a lot better than we did. A number of them made a fortune in moonshining and bootlegging. Mr. Carl Green was one of them. He started out moonshining; then he'd contract it out to other men, especially down around Corinth, where he was from. Back in the forties and fifties, when Phenix City was wide open, he sold thousands of gallons over there every year. Sometimes he'd haul it over in a tanker truck. He went on to become a millionaire, and after he became a road commissioner, he just about ran the county.

We didn't work scared all the time, but when somebody nearby got caught, we were afraid we might be next. I always thought I could outrun a deer if a revenuer got after me. But one time we were making whiskey over on the Reynolds' place across from Macedonia Church, and the owner found out somehow what we were doing. One day we looked up and saw a man coming straight toward us through the woods. It turned out to be the owner, but I thought it was the Law and I started running and got about a hundred yards away and my knees turned to jelly and I fell over into a ditch. The man walked up, saw me folded up in the ditch, smiled down at me, and walked away. If he'd been the Law, I'd have been caught. He didn't care what we were doing on his land, but you better believe we moved our still that night to another location. Most landowners didn't mind, but we felt better if they didn't know. It's safer to make whiskey on your own land or on the land of an absentee landowner, like the paper companies.

Daddy got sent off to prison one time for making moonshine. The revenue agents found a still on our place and caught the old man at the still that Daddy had working for him. The man said it was Daddy's still, so they came to the house, arrested him, put him on trial, and found him guilty. He spent eight months at the federal penitentiary at Maxwell Field in Montgomery. Life was so easy there that everybody called it "the country club." He was sentenced by Judge Frank Johnson, who said, using the legal terminology, "I sentence you to the custody of the Attorney General of the United States for a period of two years." At that time—it was 1973—the attorney general of the United States was John Mitchell, who was involved in Watergate and the Nixon scandals and wound up in the same prison Daddy was in. Daddy used to say, "Well, I got the last laugh on Attorney General Mitchell. He may have had custody of me for a while, but when I left Maxwell Field, that SOB took my bed."

When a moonshiner got caught, it was usually because a

jealous neighbor told on him. We called it being "turned up." It was almost impossible for a revenuer to find a still without being told where it was. Daddy said, "That man that turned me up ain't nothing in the world but a damn pimp." The "pimp" was usually another moonshiner who was trying to eliminate competition.

I was soon a part of the family business, assisting Daddy and his other helper, my older brother Spooky. One man could have run a small still by himself, but it would have been hard work because of the logistics of the operation. You had to hide the still way back in the woods. You had to carry all the sugar and rye and barrels and bottles in and out. You had to tote all that stuff a long way because you couldn't have a road leading up to the still. It would have been a dead giveaway and led the revenue agents right up to your illegal operation. When he didn't have enough help from his sons, Daddy would hire other help, and sometimes he'd go in with a partner. An old black man named Hundun helped him a long time.

Daddy had his business all set up long before I became involved. He had already developed his policies and procedures—from the production to the marketing. We never sold our whiskey to the consumer but to middlemen who were called bootleggers. They bought it from us by the gallon and would break it up to put into pints or half pints or Coca-Cola bottles for retail sales in little country stores or nightclubs. They would always arrange to make a pickup at night. They'd come to our house, pay Daddy for what they had ordered, and he'd take them to where we had stashed it in the woods. The biggest bootlegger that Daddy dealt with was a black man in Bullock County, a big landowner up near Three Notch; but he sold most of his whiskey to bootleggers in such nearby counties as Macon, Tallapoosa, and Barbour—all of which used to be dry. Moonshine was also popular in wet counties because it was cheaper and better tasting—at least, ours was—than the legal brands. Like most moonshiners, Daddy drank little or none of his own product. When I asked him why, he said, "Son, we make this whiskey to sell, not to drink."

And he sold it to bootleggers who demanded the very best. They bought from Daddy because they knew he would deliver it.

6

DADDY'S CONECUH RIDGE RECIPE

This is how Daddy went about making his prized moonshine that was the choice of discriminating drinkers. It is not complicated. Distilling is basically a very simple process. It's just a matter of turning steam to liquid.

It involves, first, the construction of a still. The best stills are made out of copper, which is a good conductor of heat and isn't poisonous like lead. Daddy's stills were always made of copper. You've got to keep lead away from whiskey. Even when soldering the parts of a still together with lead, you have to make sure that the lead stays outside the seams. Whiskey must never be exposed to lead, or you'll wind up with customers with lead poisoning that could be fatal. Some men used galvanized steel and even leaded car radiators for condensers. They're the ones who made the moonshine that could blind or kill a drinker with lead poisoning. They're the ones who gave moonshining a bad rap, and Daddy had no use for them.

A still looks like a big box. Ours were usually fourteen to sixteen inches high, three or four feet wide, five or six feet long. You cut a hole in the middle of the top cover and put a collar over it. You fit pipes into the collar and they go to the thumper. Then you have the condenser, which is a bunch of coiled copper that's encased in sheet copper. That's what changes the steam to liquid.

Now we come to the actual operation. This is the process

that Daddy used to make his superior whiskey. To begin with, you have to have a good supply of good water. We'll start with the location of his distillery and the nearby water source that provides the whiskey with its most basic and crucial ingredient. Conecuh Ridge runs from northern Pike County through the western end of Bullock County at High Ridge all the way to Union Springs, coming down by the country club and then out the Peachburg Road along Chunnunuggee Ridge, where the Conecuh River is sourced by the Springs of Conecuh.

It's the fresh, pure water of these springs and the small branches and streams that feed into the Conecuh River as it meanders slowly and sluggishly southward—all filtered by the sandy soil of the ridgelands—that produces the main and vital ingredient for good moonshine whiskey. All over Bullock County and Pike County there are artesian wells that bubble up from the high aquifer that underlies the land. But you can't put an illegal distillery out in plain sight. You have to find a source of good water in a remote, inaccessible, naturally camouflaged location—a place no revenue agent can find.

Daddy would put his still on one of those sand ridges in a thicket of woods at a spring head, which he would dig out to form a reservoir—a pool six to eight feet square and about three feet deep—of the clearest, prettiest, sparklingest water you've ever seen—the best-tasting water this side of Paradise.

I can't overemphasize the importance of water. You can't make whiskey without water and you can't make good whiskey without good water. By good water, I mean it has to be clean and pure. That's the kind of water we still have in abundance on Conecuh Ridge. It is water that tastes good because it starts out with the proper balance of minerals and then is naturally filtered through layers of clean, white sand.

At Daddy's still as soon as the pool filled up, the water would become clear and pure, and it would be flowing constantly. You can't use stale, stagnant water. Daddy would locate his still below the water supply and run a plastic pipe with a drop of six to eight feet from the reservoir to the still. Gravity will keep it flowing. He always put a strainer on the intake opening of the pipe to keep out leaves and other trash. That's the moonshiner's version of running water. You could tote your water from the reservoir to the still—and I have carried thousands of gallons that way—but it's a lot easier to pipe it down.

You start the process with fifty-five gallon metal drums that cooking oil or mayonnaise or pickles were stored in before they were put in smaller containers for retail. We could buy them for two dollars a piece. We washed them out thoroughly to remove any food taste. We usually cooked off three barrels at a time. In those barrels you put some starter—a yeast culture with grain that has already swollen and fermented. It's like a starter for sourdough bread.

We'd put about a bushel of rye and enough water to cover it in each barrel, plus a slip of sugar—about sixty pounds. We'd get our rye and sugar at the Farmers' Exchange in Union Springs and sometimes the local grocery store. Most of the rye we used was grown in the Dakotas because it had bigger grain than locally grown rye. Oh sure, the merchants we bought from knew exactly what we were going to do with the rye and also the large amounts of sugar. All our suppliers knew the name of the game. A lot of the business the little country stores did in those days was with moonshiners. We were helping them and they were helping us.

The rye went on the bottom of the barrel; then we'd cover it with water and starter or yeast, and let the rye swell for a

Two views of illegal distilleries of the type common to Bullock County, Alabama, during the period when Clyde May was operating, though these are not his. These photos were obtained from retired revenue agent Tom Allison.

couple of days. While it was swelling we'd set up the still close to the water supply, fill it with water, and put a propane burner under it and heat that water until it got lukewarm; then we'd pour it over the rye and add the sugar. That's when it starts fermenting. We had to keep the barrels warm—though not hot—so that they'd continue working. That wasn't a problem in the summertime, but in winter we'd pack pine straw around the barrel drums to keep them warm. We'd let that mixture ferment or "work" for maybe five days; then we'd put the mixture in the still and cook it. The sour mash that we dipped out of the barrel and poured into the still smelled like beer, so we called it beer.

The propane gas heat under the still starts the beer to cook. The first thing that boils is the alcohol, which turns to steam that goes down through those coils round and round until it hits cold water and is condensed into liquid. Daddy always made a biscuit dough out of White Lily Flour and sealed the top to keep the steam from escaping. He insisted on White Lily because, he said, "It's the best."

There were pipes that led from the still over to a thumper, which was a small reservoir, and from the thumper to the condenser, which runs through water that condenses the steam alcohol into liquid alcohol, which we caught in wide-mouthed gallon jugs. Daddy checked each jug to make sure the beads indicated the right strength. When the whiskey drips into the jug, it is ready to drink. It is white or clear as water; and that's the way most of our moonshine—or white lightning—was sold and consumed. Whiskey gets its color when it's put in a charred keg and allowed to age.

We'd run all the contents of the three barrels or drums through that same process. The first gallon you run is the strongest, which means it has the highest alcohol content. When the grain starts getting weak, you dip some of it off and replace it with fresh grain to keep the alcohol content high. We could also blend the whiskey from all the runs to make the proof about the same in each jug. We could tell that the whiskey in each jug was about the same proof by checking the number and size of the beads. We shook the jug to make the beads form. We could also check the strength by tasting the whiskey in each jug, but we didn't usually need to do that. You see, Daddy had quality control throughout the process. Most of our moonshine was about sixty per cent alcohol or around 120 proof. By contrast, commercial whiskey bought in a liquor store is only eighty or ninety proof.

Daddy's whiskey was the best for a lot of reasons. He maintained high standards all the time. He didn't make rot-gut whiskey. You could say he took moonshining to a higher level. I think he made it an art. Daddy was fanatical about cleanliness. His ingredients were the best—the best water, the best grain. Some distillers grind up the whole grain of corn or barley and rye because it hastens the fermentation process, but to Daddy that was a shortcut. He always used the whole grain so that it could swell and ferment naturally.

After he made a run, he thoroughly cleaned out the still and all the equipment. The sour mash had to be covered when it was fermenting so that nothing could get into it—no animals, no stray trash, nothing to dilute its purity. His standards were so high he would have destroyed a whole batch if it didn't come up to par. He would never have put his name on a gallon of whiskey that didn't meet his rigorous standards. Every gallon had to have the proper bead count, the right clarity and color, and, if necessary, had to pass his own taste

Another "revenuer" photo from a confiscated still, this one in Pike County, south of Bullock County. This photo shows the barrels of fermenting mash. In the four barrels in the foreground, the rye "cap" has sunk and the mash is clear, indicating that it is ready to run.

test. He didn't try to squeeze out an extra gallon or two from a run because the proof gets lower the more you run it. He was constantly checking the bead on the whiskey to see if the bead was holding up. When it dropped too low, it was flat, like a Coke that has been left open too long and has lost its fizz. He'd say, "All right, boys, that's enough. The bead has fallen." So he'd stop the run.

Daddy said, "There's only good whiskey and bad whiskey. I make only good whiskey. If I ever made a bad run of whiskey, no one ever knew it. I poured it out. No one ever had a chance to drink it."

As a rule Daddy didn't drink his own whiskey, but one time, to prove a point, he did. A man came to buy some moonshine and started haggling over the price. Then the man said, "Clyde, that's just not good whiskey. I've drunk a lot better." Well, that set Daddy off. To prove that it was good, he started drinking it and got silly and tipsy. Finally, Mama said, "Clyde, you've had too much. You've made your point. Now go on to bed and sleep it off."

Daddy had such a reputation for making good whiskey that even the revenuers said they hated to pour it out when they broke up one of his stills. I've even heard that sometimes they'd keep back a couple of gallons for themselves. One revenuer told me, "You know, your daddy's whiskey was so good, it always brought a tear to my eye when I had to pour it out."

Daddy's best moonshine was his special Christmas whiskey. And that's the kind that I'm going to produce. Most of his whiskey he sold fresh off the still, but he always aged his Christmas whiskey. Aging it in charred oak barrels will improve its taste and appearance, giving the whiskey a caramel flavor and color. Daddy would also put some charred oak chips in the barrel to make it mellow and smooth and to give it a kind of vanilla and caramel flavor and color. He'd char white oak chips by putting them in the fireplace or on a grill and starting them to burn, then putting the fire out when they get dark. The heat releases the resins in the wood so that when you put it in the whiskey, it comes out. It made the whiskey smoother. He would get some tart Washington State apples, core them, remove the seeds, and slowly dry them in the oven, then he'd add the dried pieces to the raw whiskey in the barrels and leave them there for a couple of weeks. Daddy said, "This helps to mellow the whiskey. It takes away the bite and makes it smooth and mellow." Daddy used to say, "The natural way is Nature's way."

We made whiskey throughout the year during all seasons, but Daddy said the best whiskey is made in the fall when the sap is falling in the trees. When he aged his special whiskey, he'd put it up in the fall or winter and let it age for maybe a year. It ages faster in the summer because of the heat. It doesn't take as long to age whiskey in the American South as it does in the North or in Scotland or other colder climates. Daddy thought a year was long enough to age whiskey, but that was a year in Alabama's climate.

So he always put aside some batches that he made then and poured those special runs into kegs to age and mellow. Man, oh man, after it had aged and drawn out the flavors from the keg and the chips and the apples, he would siphon it out in gallon jugs, and it was ready for the King's table. That was his Christmas whiskey. The man who was lucky enough to get a bottle had a Merry Christmas that lasted into the New Year. And that is the whiskey I'm calling Clyde May's Conecuh Ridge.

7

THE LEGACY OF CLYDE MAY

Daddy was a good man and lived a good life. He died in January of 1990 and his funeral at Macedonia Baptist Church was the biggest I've ever been to. I don't think he realized how many people he had touched and how much they admired him. I've had total strangers come up to me and say, "You're Clyde May's son, aren't you? Well, I just want you to know how lucky you were to have a daddy like him." One example of the respect that people had for him was evident when one of his pallbearers, Tommy Paulk, wrote Mama a letter immediately after Daddy's funeral. In it, he said,

> I would like to thank you for bestowing upon me the honor of service as pallbearer for Clyde. It is my hope that when six men carry me in like fashion, one of them will feel for me the respect I have for Clyde.
>
> Clyde May was loved and respected for many reasons, and each of us has his/her own. I would like to tell you mine:
>
> If Clyde May said he would do something, he did it. His reliability was absolute; he never came with excuses, even when excuses were plentiful and just. There are few people in this world about whom it can truly be said, "His word is his bond, his handshake is worth more than all the signed contracts any lawyer can create." Clyde May was such a man.

The weight of Clyde's death will never go completely away, and there is nothing any of us can do to make up for his loss. But there may be a way we can make that weight a little lighter. Maybe we can adopt for ourselves some of the attributes that Clyde has shown us are indeed humanly possible. And maybe we can teach our children and our children's children what it means to have it said about us: "His word is his bond."

I hope your sadness can be eased by the awareness that without death there can be no life and by the awareness of the gratitude we all feel for having shared in Clyde's life. I am grateful that Clyde May lived. I am grateful that I knew him. And I am proud that he called me "friend."

Yes, Daddy was a genuine man of his word, generous and trustworthy with a heart as big as a watermelon. And now I believe he made the best whiskey in the whole South. At least, I've never tasted any better.

This is my heritage and I'm proud of it all. During Daddy's lifetime we could never talk about moonshining, but I'm thankful that now we can. I'm thankful that I can pay tribute to a man like my daddy who cared so much for his family he would risk his own freedom. And I'm thankful that he was a craftsman of high standards, a man who put out a product that he was proud of and would stand behind. I'm thankful that we can now recognize someone like him.

Some of the older fellows in Bullock County still have a few bottles of Daddy's whiskey hidden away. Recently I looked out the window of my office in Union Springs and saw an old man coming up the steps. He came in and put down a Seagrams's Crown Royal bottle on my desk, and said, "Kenny, this is the last whiskey I got from your Daddy fifteen years

Mr. and Mrs. Clyde May and Debbie, ca. 1980.

ago, and I want you to have it." I still have it. It's almost like something sacred.

Why do people like whiskey? Why do people like anything that is soothing, smooth, and mellow? An old man once tried to explain to me the pleasure he got from a plug of chewing tobacco. "A good chew of tobacco just soothes me down," he said, "and makes me happy with the world."

That's the way it is with good whiskey. Real whiskey drinkers love the taste of it before they feel any of the effects, before they get a buzz or a glow or a high. People like to drink whiskey to relax, to unwind, to get rid of tension, to sleep better. Good whiskey is truly "the waters of life," which is what the word *whiskey* means in Gaelic. In proper amounts, it will intensify any pleasure. And what is the secret of Daddy's special recipe? I think, finally, it's like any of life's supreme pleasures. It's a mystery you can't define or describe. It is something you experience. You participate in its mystery when you drink some of my Conecuh Ridge. The secret is in the sipping.

Conecuh Ridge Distillery
101B West Elm Street
Troy, Alabama 36081
www.crwhiskey.com

From the promotional brochure for Conecuh Ridge whiskey.

Index

Because the narrator, Kenny May, and his father, Lewis Clyde May, are present throughout this narrative, most of their index entries are restricted to photographs. All the placenames, unless otherwise indicated, are in Bullock County or elsewhere in Alabama.

About the Author

A native of Union Springs, Alabama, Wade Hall has lived since 1962 in Louisville, where he taught English and chaired the English and humanities/arts programs at Kentucky Southern College and Bellarmine College. He has also taught at the University of Illinois and the University of Florida. He holds degrees from Troy State University (B.S.), the University of Alabama (M. A.), and the University of Illinois (Ph.D.). He served for two years in the U.S. Army in the mid-fifties. His most recent books include *A Visit with Harlan Hubbard; High Upon a Hill: A History of Bellarmine College,* and *A Song in Native Pastures: Randy Atcher's Life in Country Music.* Other writings include hundreds of articles, poems, essays and reviews published in historical and scholarly journals as well as popular magazines and newspapers. He served as editor of the *Kentucky Poetry Review* for more than fifteen years and hosted a weekly interview program over the public television affiliate in Louisville. In 1967 he received the Literary Award of the Alabama Library Association for "Distinguished Contribution to Alabama's Literary Heritage." In 1988 *The Rest of the Dream* was recognized as one of the outstanding books published on race relations in the United States. His *Conecuh People* was adapted for the stage by New York playwright Ty Adams in 2001 and premiered at Troy State University in January 2002. For the past three decades he has aggressively collected books about the South, picture post cards, photography, American sheet music and recordings, folk art, quilts, and American letters and diaries, including a large component of Civil War manuscripts. These are being deposited at the University of Alabama, the University of Kentucky, the Kentucky History Center, Troy State University, the Birmingham Museum of Art, the J. B. Speed Art Museum, and the Columbus (Ga.) Museum.

CPSIA information can be obtained
at www.ICGtesting.com
Printed in the USA
LVHW111628221122
733807LV00004B/747